NATIONAL GEOGRAPHIC

Exploring Ecosystems

Kate Boehm Jerome

PICTURE CREDITS

Cover (front), 5 (bottom), 9, 25 (bottom right), 30 (top right), 31 (top right), The Image Bank/Getty Images; 1, Roy Toft/National Geographic Image Collection; 2-3, Larry Lee Photography/Corbis; 4-5 (top), 8 (top left), 20 (bottom), 22 (bottom), 31 (bottom left), 34 (second from bottom), Royalty-Free Corbis; 4-5 (bottom), 8 (top right), 18 (top and bottom), 25 (top right), 35 (second from bottom), Raymond Gehman/National Geographic Image Collection; 5 (top), 35 (bottom), Wolfgang Kaehler/Corbis; 6-7, Digital Vision/Getty Images; 8 (bottom left), Comstock Images/Getty Images; 8 (bottom right), 10 (bottom), Photodisc/Getty Images; 10 (top), Dex Image, Royalty Free/Getty; 11 (top), 30 (top left), National Geographic/Warren Marr/Panoramic Images; 11 (middle), Ross Pictures/Corbis; 11 (bottom), Allen Prier/Panoramic Images/NGSImages.com; 12, 25 (bottom left), 35 (second from top), D. Robert & Lorri Franz/Corbis; 13, 25 (top left), 30 (bottom left), 34 (top), W. Perry Conway/Corbis; 14, 31 (middle left), Raymond Gehman/Corbis; 15, 30 (bottom right), Gary Braasch/Corbis; 16-17, Stone/Getty Images; 19 (top left), Cindy Kassab/Corbis; 19 (top right), Photographer's Choice/Getty Images; 19 (bottom left), 31 (middle right), 34 (second from top), Darrell Gulin/Corbis; 19 (bottom right), Ted Horowitz/Corbis; 20 (top), Nicole Duplaix/National Geographic Image Collection; 21, 29, 35 (top), Paul A. Sounders/Corbis; 22 (top), William Weber/Visuals Unlimited; 23 (top), 31 (bottom right), Joe McDonald/ Corbis; 23 (bottom), 31 (top left), Mark L. Stephenson/Corbis; 26, US Fish & Wildlife; 27, Art Wolfe/Stone/Getty Images; 28, Joel Sartore/National Geographic Image Collection; 32, Gary W. Carter/Corbis; 34 (middle), Jose Fuste Raga/Corbis; 34 (bottom), Ned Therrien/Visuals Unlimited; 36, Digital Vision/Foto Search

Produced through the worldwide resources of the National Geographic Society, John M. Fahey, Jr., President and Chief Executive Officer; Gilbert M. Grosvenor, Chairman of the Board; Nina D. Hoffman, Executive Vice President and President, Books and Education Publishing Group.

PREPARED BY NATIONAL GEOGRAPHIC SCHOOL PUBLISHING

Ericka Markman, Senior Vice President and President, Children's Books and Education Publishing Group; Steve Mico, Senior Vice President, Editorial Director, Publisher; Francis Downey, Executive Editor; Richard Easby, Editorial Manager; Bea Jackson, Director of Layout and Design; Jim Hiscott, Design Manager; Cynthia Olson, Art Director; Margaret Sidlosky, Illustrations Director; Matt Wascavage, Manager of Publishing Services; Sean Philpotts, Jane Ponton, Production Managers; Ted Tucker, Production Specialist.

MANUFACTURING AND QUALITY CONTROL

Christopher A. Liedel, Chief Financial Officer; Phillip L. Schlosser, Director; Clifton M. Brown III, Manager

CONSULTANTS AND REVIEWERS

Kefyn M. Catley, Ph.D., Assistant Professor of Science Education, Department of Teaching and Learning, Peabody College, Assistant Professor of Biology, Vanderbilt University, Research Associate, Division of Invertebrate Zoology, American Museum of Natural History, New York

Julie Edmonds, Associate Director, Carnegie Academy for Science Education, Carnegie Institution of Washington

◀ **Living and nonliving things make up this ecosystem in Wyoming.**

Contents

Build Background   **4**
Survival Skills

1 **Understand the Big Idea**   **6**
Staying Alive

2 **Take a Closer Look**   **16**
Footsteps Through the Forest

3 **Make Connections**   **24**

Extend Learning   **30**

Glossary   **34**

Index   **36**

BOOK DEVELOPMENT
Amy Sarver

BOOK DESIGN/PHOTO RESEARCH
3R1 Group, Inc.

Published by the National Geographic Society
Washington, D.C. 20036-4688

Product No. 4T60300

ISBN: 0-7922-5409-0

Printed in Mexico

11 10 09 08 07
10 9 8 7 6 5 4 3

SURVIVAL SKILLS

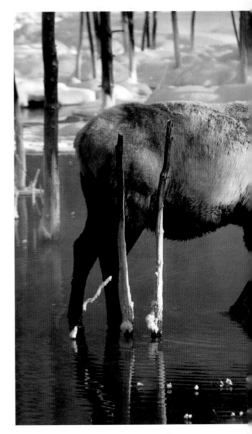

▲ **The elk needs water to live.**

It is not easy for plants and animals to stay alive, or **survive.** They need things to help them live. Animals need food, water, air, and shelter. Plants need air, light, water, and soil. All living things need other living things and nonliving things to help them survive.

Look at the pictures.

- What living things do you see?
- What nonliving things do you see?
- How do nonliving things help the animals and plants survive?

....

survive – to stay alive

▲ **Plants need sunlight to grow.**

▲ This lizard eats a cactus.

▲ Baby birds are protected in a nest made of twigs.

Big Idea
Ecosystems are made of living and nonliving things.

Set Purpose
Learn about the living and nonliving things in ecosystems.

Stayi

What is an ecosystem?

How do living things share an ecosystem?

ng Alive

Think of all the things you need to stay alive. You need air to breathe. You need water to drink. You need food to eat. So where do you get these things? All living things get what they need from their **ecosystem.** An ecosystem includes the living and nonliving things in an area.

ecosystem – all the living and nonliving things in an area

Air

Water

Sunlight

Soil

Nonliving Things Are Important

All living things need nonliving things to live. Nonliving things are not alive. Here are some nonliving things that plants and animals need to survive.

- air
- water
- sunlight
- soil

▲ These bears need the plants, water, and air in their ecosystem.

Nonliving + Living = Ecosystem

Most living things also need other living things. Different kinds of plants and animals need one another.

An ecosystem is made of both the living and nonliving things in an area. Look at the photograph above. The bears and plants are living things. The water and air are nonliving things. They are all part of the same ecosystem.

▲ A pond is a small ecosystem.

Small in Size

Ecosystems can be small. For example, a pond is an ecosystem. It can have fish, frogs, and plants. The water, rocks, and soil are also part of the ecosystem. Even tiny living things too small to be seen are part of the pond ecosystem.

▶ A frog can be part of a pond ecosystem.

Desert

Rain forest

Tundra

▲ Some ecosystems are large.

Big Is Beautiful, Too

Ecosystems can also be large. For example,
a big, sandy desert is an ecosystem. So is a
tree-filled rain forest and a cold Arctic tundra.
These ecosystems can stretch for miles and
miles. The pictures above show these large
ecosystems.

▲ These prairie dogs are part of this ecosystem's prairie dog population.

What Is a Population?

Ecosystems provide homes for many living things. A group of plants or animals of the same kind that live in the same area is called a **population.**

A prairie ecosystem can have many populations. Populations of plants live there. Rabbits, snakes, and prairie dogs may live there, too.

....

population – a group of plants or animals of the same kind that live in the same area

Burrow

▲ This burrowing owl made its nest in an empty prairie dog hole.

Populations Are Connected

The populations that live in an area are all connected. For example, burrowing owls build nests in **burrows.** Burrows are holes in the ground where animals live. It is not easy for owls to dig. What do they do?

The owls can use burrows made by prairie dogs or other animals. This means owls and prairie dogs can both live in the same ecosystem. And they use some of the same **resources,** or materials that come from nature.

burrow – a hole in the ground where an animal lives

resource – a natural material that living things use

▲ A forest fire kills trees and changes the populations living in the area.

Changing Populations

Changes to ecosystems can make populations change. Sometimes the changes are natural. Think about a forest fire. It can kill trees. Many animals can lose their homes. They may not be able to find food. Then the animals must move to another place. Or they die.

A **drought** can also cause changes. A drought is when rain does not fall for a long time. Without water, land can become very hard and dry. Then plants and animals may die.

....
drought – a long period without much rainfall

14

Populations in a forest change when people cut down trees.

Human Change

People can also change ecosystems. Some changes can make populations smaller. This can happen when people cut down too many trees. The populations of trees get smaller. The populations of plants and animals that lived in or near the trees also get smaller.

People can also cause changes that make populations larger. This can happen when people protect ecosystems. For example, some forests are protected. No one can cut down trees or hunt animals. The populations of trees and other living things get larger.

Stop and Think!

What nonliving things can make up ecosystems?

15

Recap
Describe the living and nonliving things that can be found in an ecosystem.

Set Purpose
Explore the living and nonliving things that make up a forest ecosystem.

Footsteps Through th

A forest seems quiet and still. But do not be fooled. In a forest, you are surrounded by living and nonliving things. Together they make up the forest ecosystem.

FOREST

In the Forest

You are deep in the forest. Trees tower above you. Limbs stretch across the sky. Sunlight bathes the treetops. Fallen leaves crunch under your feet. Birdsongs fill the air. Squirrels leap from tree to tree.

The plants and animals may catch your eye. Yet nonliving things are here, too. Sunlight hits the trees. There are also the soil, rocks, and water. All of these are important parts of a forest ecosystem.

▲ Squirrels are living things in the forest ecosystem.

▼ Water and rocks are nonliving things in the forest ecosystem.

Losing Leaves

Many trees are **deciduous.** That means that they lose their leaves. Trees begin to lose their leaves in the **fall.** At this time, many leaves change colors. Leaves can be brilliant yellows, reds, and oranges. But these colors do not last long. Soon the leaves drop to the ground. The cold winter will begin soon.

deciduous – having leaves that fall off every year

fall – the season of the year that follows summer

Four Seasons in Deciduous Forests

Spring | Summer

Fall | Winter

Look Up!

You do not have to look far to find the animals in the forest. The trees are alive with birds and squirrels. There are hundreds of different kinds of insects.

Did you know that almost everything in the forest has a use? Even dying trees make useful homes. Red-headed woodpeckers make holes in the wood. This is how they find insects to eat. These holes then become perfect homes for other small animals.

▲ This woodpecker finds insects by making a hole in the tree.

▼ Treetops are homes to many kinds of animals.

Look Down!

Even the **forest floor** is full of life. Some populations are so small you cannot see them. Tiny living things live in and on the soil. They break down leaves and dead trees. This helps new plants to grow.

Many plants on the forest floor grow well in shade. That is good! Why? The tall trees of the forest often keep sunlight from reaching the forest floor.

....

forest floor – the ground within a forest

▼ **Many plants live on the forest floor.**

Under the Ground

You might spot a chipmunk running across a log. But this little animal spends most of its time underground. A chipmunk digs lots of tunnels. Some tunnels are over nine meters (30 feet) long.

Moles live underground, too. These forest animals dig all of their lives. Their digging helps mix air and other things into the forest soil.

▼ **Chipmunks dig tunnels in the ground.**

▼ **A mole digs through the forest floor.**

Night Life

Underground animals are not the only ones that are busy in the dark. Plenty of forest animals use the nighttime hours to hunt and move around.

Owls hunt at night. They listen carefully for the sounds of small animals. If an animal gets too close, the owl flies to catch it. Raccoons can also see well in the dark. They look for food at night. There are many ways that animals meet their needs in the forest.

▲ The owl flies from forest trees when hunting.

▼ The raccoon searches for food on the forest floor.

Stop and Think!

What living and nonliving things can be part of a forest ecosystem?

CONNECT WHAT YOU HAVE LEARNED

Exploring Ecosystems

All plants and animals get what they need from an ecosystem. An ecosystem can be as small as a pond, or as large as a desert.

Here are some ideas you learned about ecosystems.

- Ecosystems are made of living and nonliving things.
- All living things need nonliving things to survive.
- Plants or animals of the same kind that live in the same area are called populations.
- Populations in an area depend on one another.

Check What You Have Learned

How do nonliving things help these animals and plants survive?

▲ Beavers use dead trees to make their homes.

▲ Plants need light to live and grow.

▲ Populations of prairie dogs make burrows
  in soil.

▲ These bears need the living and nonliving things
  in their ecosystem.

What Is a Habitat?

A habitat is a place where a plant or animal lives in an ecosystem. Students and teachers across the country are making schoolyard habitats. These are areas on school grounds for wildlife. Here animals and plants have everything they need to live.

If you want to make a schoolyard habitat, the U.S. Fish and Wildlife Service can help. Its Schoolyard Habitat program helps students and teachers plan and build habitats for many kinds of plants and animals.

▼ These students are making a schoolyard habitat.

▲ Wetlands are important to many living things.

Wet and Wild

Wetlands are areas where the ground is soaked with water. Many kinds of plants and animals live in these wet areas. Some people want to fill in wetlands to put up buildings. But wildlife experts do not think this is a good idea. Why? Many living things in the wetlands could be harmed.

Wetlands are also important to ocean animals. Many ocean animals have their babies in wetlands along the coast. So the wetlands are important to many kinds of living things.

Wild Wolves

Two hundred years ago, red wolves roamed the forests of the eastern United States. But by the late 1960s, only a few wolves were left.

Wildlife experts captured these wolves. They were protected while they had babies. Then the wolves and their babies were let loose in the forests.

The red wolf is beginning to make a comeback in the wild. It is a slow process. But the red wolf has been saved from dying out completely.

▼ **Populations of red wolves are now getting larger in the wild.**

▲ **This moose lives very close to these homes in Alaska.**

New Neighbors

Can you imagine finding a moose on your front porch? Sometimes animals get a little too close for comfort. Why?

As cities grow, many animals lose their natural homes. When this happens, some animals look for places to live near people. This can be dangerous. City planners and animal experts try to solve the problem. They look for ways to protect wild animals as well as people living in the cities.

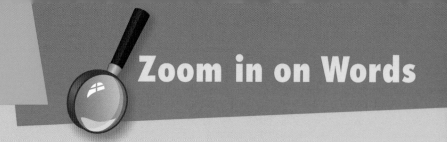
Many kinds of words are used in this book. Here you will learn about nouns. You will also learn about verbs.

Nouns

A noun is a word that names a person, animal, place, or thing. A sentence can have more than one noun. Find the nouns below. Then use each noun in your own sentence.

The **desert** is a large **ecosystem.**

Bears are living **things.**

Some **owls** build underground **burrows.**

Cutting down **trees** can change an **ecosystem.**

Verbs

A verb is a word that shows action. Find the verbs below. Use each verb in your own sentence.

The raccoon **searches** for food.

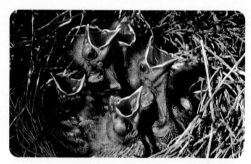

The nest **protects** the baby birds.

A forest fire **kills** trees.

During fall, green leaves of deciduous trees **change** color.

In a forest, treetops **tower** above you.

This owl **flies** at night.

Research and Write

Write About Ecosystems

Choose an ecosystem to research. Find out about ways to protect the plants and animals that live in that ecosystem. Write a letter to a lawmaker about your ideas.

Research

Collect books and reference materials, or go online.

Read and Take Notes

As you read, take notes and draw pictures.

Write

Write a letter that describes the ecosystem you researched. Explain ways that plants and animals can be protected in an ecosystem. Then tell why you think protecting this ecosystem is important.

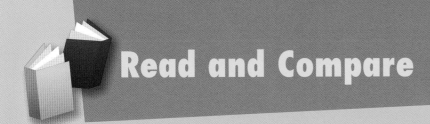

Read and Compare

Read More About Exploring Ecosystems

Find and read other books about ecosystems. As you read, think about these questions.

- What makes up an ecosystem?
- What do plants and animals need to survive?
- How can ecosystems change?

Books to Read

▲ Read about different kinds of ecosystems.

▲ Read about how scientists classify living things.

▲ Read about the features of many kinds of animals.

Glossary

burrow (page 13)
A hole in the ground where an animal lives
This owl lives in a burrow.

KEY CONCEPT

deciduous (page 19)
Having leaves that fall off every year
Deciduous trees lose their leaves in the fall.

drought (page 14)
A long period without much rainfall
A drought makes land hard and dry.

KEY CONCEPT

ecosystem (page 7)
All the living and nonliving things in an area
All living things get what they need from an ecosystem.

fall (page 19)
The season of the year that follows summer
Leaves can turn yellow, red, and orange during fall.

forest floor (page 21)
The ground within a forest
Many kinds of plants grow on the forest floor.

population (page 12)
A group of plants or animals of the same kind that
live in the same area
A population of prairie dogs lives in a prairie ecosystem.

resource (page 13)
A natural material that living things use
Water is a resource that living things need to survive.

survive (page 4)
To stay alive
The lizard survives by eating food.

Index

burrow	13, 25, 30, 34
deciduous	19, 31, 34
desert	11, 24, 30
drought	14, 34
ecosystem	6–7, 9–18, 23–26, 30, 32–35
fall	19, 31, 34
forest	15–23, 28, 31
forest fire	14, 31
forest floor	21–23, 35
habitat	26
population	12–15, 21, 24–25, 28–29, 35
rain forest	11
resource	13, 35
survive	4, 8, 24, 33, 35
tundra	11